On My Mind

Kerri-Alice Brown

BookLeaf Publishing

Presentation by *BookLeaf Publishing*

Web: www.bookleafpub.com

E-mail: info@bookleafpub.com

ISBN: 9789357440547

First edition 2023

Masquerade

I have a side to me that no one knows
No one can see it
I keep it hidden
Deep down
dark thoughts lurk
I wonder
Am I a good person
Everybody tells me that I am
But what if I'm not
What if it is all an act

But what if everyone is like that
Showing a mask to everyone else
And hiding who they truly are
We seek acceptance
And fear rejection
We alter the mask
Depending on who is seeing it
It is not one size fits all

It is easy to get lost behind the mask
Do I even know who I truly am?

Seasons

In spring the world is new,
You explore all your senses,
You cry and scream and laugh,
You feel a soothing embrace.

In summer the world seems much smaller,
You look down on others,
You see what others want you to see,
A hot pressure surrounds you.

In autumn the world starts to slow down,
You have seen spring and summer pass,
The warmth they brought you is now distant,
You accept that winter is approaching.

In winter the world becomes cold,
You have slowed more since autumn,
The ache begins to set it,
The cold takes you over.

Picture Perfect

Sun beams through the sky,
shimmering down as rays,
trickling down like rain.
Through the trees, life flows,
all living things connected,
through nature's beauty.

Underneath the Cherry Blossoms

Orange hues burn into the sky
reflected along the river.
Wilting cherry blossom trees line the bank.
Little pink raindrops
floating on the calmness of the river.
Stillness reflecting the distant mountain.
The barren bridge holding only ghosts.

The Seed of Christmas

5

Whistling winter wind,
Frozen droplets underfoot,
Tall fir trees billow.

Hustle and Bustle

6

You walk always
forwards, through
the grey smog.
Your reflection
everywhere, always
watching, following.
Surrounding sounds
deafening, beeping
screaming, honking.
Isolated in the crowd.

Sharp as a Thorn

Blue skies above pierced by
tip of jarring mountain.

Cloud gathers, swarming
green moss spreading, encasing.

Rough, jagged rocks
protruding from the ground.

Sharp as an arrowhead
Sharp as a thorn.

The Pride Endures

Snarling teeth challenging all,
but there is a hierarchy
that must be followed.
The bottom can overthrow the top.
The king of the pride can be taken down
by those who were believed to pose no threat.
A new king emerges,
but evil expects evil of others.
The king is not safe.
Paranoia seeps through the pride.
The barren wasteland causes mistrust.
Fear gives way to violence.
Fighting ensues for the sake of the pride.
The victor will lead its followers to greener
pastures.

Witches Lurk Here

Stillness of night, surround us
Engulf us in a different world
Congregate together around the cracked tree
Withered leaves crumbling around us
The darkness is our home
Darkness makes us stronger
Nature empowers us
Brings life to our being
As we conjure our dreams into reality

A Time from the Past

Rotting walls with sodden tapestries
Elements weathering the ceiling
Wooden door caving in
Stepping on the cobble stones
Echoes bouncing like a symphony
Ghosts once danced here

Death Surrounds Us

Sodden grass and mud,
squelching underfoot.
Stones protruding from the ground.
Life shortened to two figures,
date of birth and date of death.
Washed away by the rain.

Heaven's Embrace

12

The day that I died,
I was alone and felt numb,
Then bundled in warmth.

Extended Family

Some say that we should only love our own
species.
But our species is dishonest.
It is difficult to trust others.

Many find comfort with our animal friends.
Furry, slimy, scaley.
No legs, 2 legs, 4 legs.
It doesn't matter whether they bark or meow or
hiss.
They provide companionship.

But they cannot stay forever.
They come into our lives and then leave us with
a gaping hole.

Plans May Fail

I feel everything
Closing in
The clouds are
Gathering in my
Thoughts so loud
I cannot stand the
Voices telling me I am
Not enough of the
Person I should be

Everything was once
So simple, I knew what
Was expected of me
To be successful and
Strong of mind but
It didn't work out that way

I will not allow this
To rule my life
I am stronger than
I give myself credit
I need to have
Faith in my goals
Faith in My life
Faith in my meaning

What do you know about...?

15

Love is conditional and yet unconditional
Faith is all encompassing but selective
Family is there in blood, but also not
Friendship is hard but rewarding

Knowledge is freeing from fear
Fear is strength
Strength is kindness
Kindness is love

Being Open

Everyone has an opinion
What is good
What is bad
Is it that simple
What about the shades of grey
What about the rainbow
Why do we judge
Why do we hate
We need to grow
We need to learn
We need to overcome
Together we are better
Kindness can save a life

Just Breathe

When the mind becomes
Loud
When the body becomes
Agitated
Breathe
In
And
Out

Take a moment to
Listen
The birds
Chirping
The trees
Rustling
And
Breathe

What can you
Smell
Are the flowers
Overpowering
Is the grass cut
Fresh
Does it clear your

Mind
Now
Breathe

Historia

1325 BC
We look on as the pharaoh is about to make his
final journey.
A journey to the afterlife.
The cult of the dead believe he will be
reincarnated as Osiris.
That remains to be seen.
We watch as the brain is removed and the organs
are placed in canopic jars.
One would think this pharaoh would have a
place in the pyramids.
But no.
He will find his eternal rest in his own tomb that
will not be discovered for thousands of years.
He will be a discovery of a lifetime.
In death, he lives on.

480 BC
He knows he has no chance of success.
300 is not enough.
What matters more than anything is making a
stand and resisting.
This all emerged from conquering and
resistance.

He will not lay down his sword and allow the
invaders to take his home and his life.
If he must lose.
If he must perish.
Then he will lead his men and die with a sword
in his hand.
He will not surrender.

866
We see a woman that is not soft and delicate.
She does not need protection.
When the men fight, so does she.
She will not hang back whilst they give
themselves, their lives.
She is strong in a way that only a woman can be.
She has the power to give life and end it.
she holds a blade in her hand as she begins her
journey.
Leaving the old for the new.
She is a conqueror.
People will not remember her name, but that
doesn't change that she is a warrior.
She will stand alongside the men as the horn is
blown.
She will fight.

1462

A man that we know is well known as a
mythical creature.
We know he is no such thing.
He is as human as he is brutal.
He is a hero to his people and a demon to
outsiders.
People would be wise to not underestimate him.
His methods are cruel, but by doing so, he saves
lives.
Perhaps there is no need for him to act as he
does.
Punish people in the way that he does.
But that is how he gained his name.
That is why he will become infamous to all
around the world.

1511-1547
We see a man so consumed with his bloodline
that he will commit unspeakable acts.
As time goes on, he will become gluttonous and
lustful.
Keen for the flesh that will bare him a son.
Betrayal will result in death.
He has heirs, but he believes one must have a
penis to rule.
To continue the name.
The legacy.
His death has the power to set a woman free.

It is not he who leaves the largest legacy.
His DAUGHTER rules with an iron fist.

1789
We can see the divide.
The rich and the poor.
The wealthy do not know the struggle and the
suffering.
The food shortages and the fear.
The rich that hide away behind their walls
cannot foresee what is to come.
The people have a voice and when they become
desperate, they will take action.
They will overthrow those they see as tyrants.
There will be no mercy as they fight for their
human rights.
No mercy as they fight for their freedom.

A Message to my Future Self

There comes a time when I must look back at
where we came from.
I see how devices have become a regular part of
life.
Reading a book.
Listening to music.
Watching a film.
All can be found on a phone.
In hindsight, we should have seen this change.
We now live in a world where the art of
conversation is dying.
A 'Hello' to a stranger is seen as odd.
I miss the day when I would look out the
window and become lost in a daydream.
Now I am glued to my phone.
I see now that life has become defined by our
technology.

Worth the Fight

One in two of us will get cancer in our lifetime.
If we do not get it, the chances are we will know
someone who has.
Or will.
It is a killer.
But cancer is not a death sentence.
Three months can become six years with
treatment.
It is not one size fits all.
But anyone who fights cancer has a strength that
we cannot truly understand.
And those we lose, we will mourn.
But we will always carry their memory.

Tranquility

What's on my island?
Freedom and escapism.
You are welcome here.